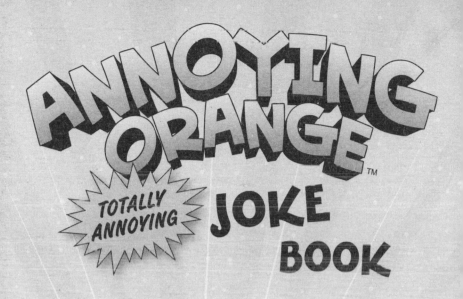

ANNOYING ORANGE™

TOTALLY ANNOYING JOKE BOOK

EGMONT
We bring stories to life

First published in Great Britain 2013 by
Egmont UK Limited
The Yellow Building, 1 Nicholas Road,
London W11 4AN

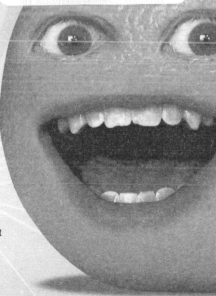

Stay safe online. Any website addresses
listed in this book are correct at the
time of going to print. However, Egmont
is not responsible for content hosted
by third parties. Please be aware that
online content can be subject to change
and websites can contain content that is
unsuitable for children. We advise that all
children are supervised when using
the internet.

ISBN 978 1 4052 6732 8
55213/3
Printed in Great Britain

PEELS OF LAUGHTER!

HEY! HEY! HEY, YOU! I'M ANNOYING ORANGE, AND THIS IS MY JOKE BOOK! I BET YOU CAN'T TELL COOL JOKES LIKE ME, CAN YOU? DON'T WORRY, I'M GOING TO HELP YOU OUT. I'M NICE LIKE THAT.

READ ON, AND I'LL HAVE YOU IN PEELS OF LAUGHTER IN NO TIME!

I SHOULD WARN YOU, THOUGH: MOST OF THESE ARE FOOD JOKES, BUT THEY'RE NOT ALL IN GOOD TASTE! HAHAHAHA!

I DON'T KNOW WHY MY FRIENDS CALL ME ANNOYING ORANGE. HMM... MAYBE IT'S BECAUSE I LOVE TO *RIND THEM UP!*

DID YOU KNOW I'M ACTUALLY PRETTY AWESOME AT TENNIS? YEAH, I'M THE *NUMBER ONE SEED!*

SOMETIMES I NEED A BIG OLD CAN OF ENERGY DRINK, WHEN I'VE *RUN OUT OF JUICE* ...

WAZZUUUP!

FRUITY FRIENDS

I'D LIKE TO SAY ALL THESE FRUIT-BASKET CASES ARE MY FRIENDS, BUT IT'S KIND OF TURNED INTO A TURF WAR IN THIS KITCHEN. YEAH, CITRUS AND THEM! HAHAHAHAHA!

THIS GUY MIGHT BE A PEAR ... BUT HE'S REALLY ONE OF A KIND! HE'S MY BEST BUDDY: HE ALWAYS HELPS ME OUT WHEN THINGS GO *PEAR-SHAPED!*

That could be the worst joke I ever heard.

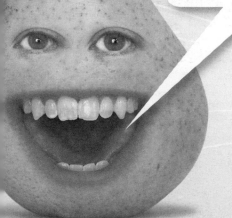

Time to hit the tyres and light the fires!

PASSION'S SUCH A ROMANTIC FRUIT — SHE LOVES *DATES*! WHEN I FIRST MET PASSION FRUIT, IT WAS *LOVE AT FIRST BITE*...

I CALL THIS GUY MIDGET APPLE 'COS HE'S A LITTLE *PIPSQUEAK*!

HE'S SO TINY YOU HAVE TO BE CAREFUL NOT TO TREAD ON HIM — YOU MIGHT MAKE *APPLE CRUMBLE*!

MARSHMALLOW'S A REAL SWEETIE — IT'S PROBABLY *ALL THAT SUGAR*!

HEY, MARSHMALLOW! WHAT DO YOU GET WHEN YOU CROSS A UNICORN WITH A BOWL OF CEREAL? *UNICORN FLAKES*!

I LOVE unicorns! And rainbows! And sunshine! And cereal! And SPRINKLES!

THAT'S GRANDPA LEMON — HE'S REALLY OLD AND REALLY BITTER. BUT HE HASN'T LOST HIS *ZEST FOR LIFE*!

GRAPEFRUIT JUST LOVES THE GYM. HE SHOULD HANG OUT WITH THE SEAFOOD, 'COS HE LOVES HIS *MUSCLES* SO MUCH! HAHAHA!

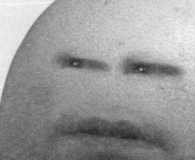

FRUITY FRIEND FUNNIES

HEY, MIDGET APPLE! IF YOU WENT SURFING YOU'D NEED TO CATCH A *MICROWAVE!* HAHAHAHA!

HEY! MIDGET APPLE, WHEN IT'S DARK DO YOU NEED A *MICROLIGHT?* HAHAHA!

Hey! That's LITTLE Apple!

HEY! HEY, APPLE! WHY ARE YOU WEARING AN APRON? YOU'RE NOT A *COOKING APPLE!*

MAN, I THOUGHT I WAS BORED — THEN A MAGGOT CHEWED ITS WAY THROUGH APPLE! NOW THAT'S WHAT I CALL *'BORED'!*

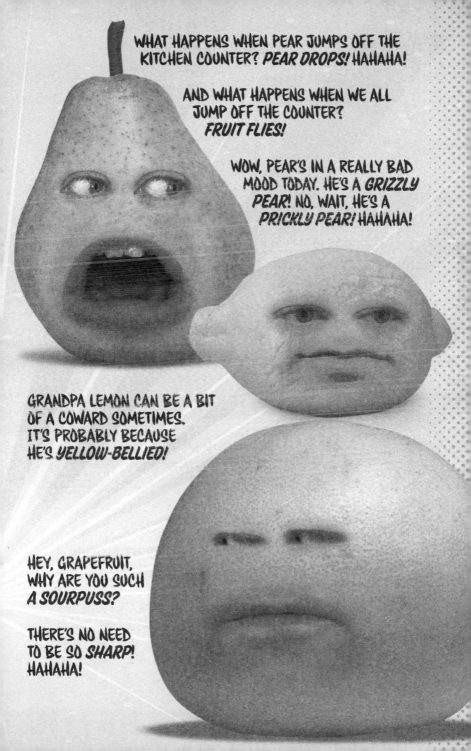

FRUIT SALAD

OH, MAN, I HATE IT WHEN THE OTHER FRUITS PUT ON A SHOW. STARFRUIT THINKS HE'S THE STAR, AND LIME'S ALWAYS STEALING THE *LIMELIGHT!*

HEY, BANANA, WHERE ARE YOU GOING? DON'T SPLIT! AREN'T YOU *PEELING WELL?*

HEY, CHERRY, STOP FOLLOWING ME AROUND! I DON'T WANT *A STALKER!*

HEY! WHAT'S BROWN, HAIRY AND WEARS SUNGLASSES? A *COCONUT ON HOLIDAY!*

EY! EY! EY! EY! EY! EY

MORE FRUIT SALAD!

HEY! WHAT DO YOU CALL LIME WHEN HE'S UNDERWATER? *SUBLIME.*

THAT MELON IS ALWAYS SO MISERABLE! WANT TO KNOW WHAT HAPPENS WHEN MELON CRIES? *MELON BAWLS!* HE'S SO *MELON-CHOLY* ... HAHAHA!

PEACH MIGHT LOOK WARM AND FUZZY, BUT SHE'S GOT A *HEART OF STONE!*

AARGH!

HEY, PINEAPPLE, GIMME A *RING SOMETIME!*

PLUM, WHEN YOU SIT IN THE BATH TOO LONG DO YOU GO ALL *PRUNY?*

HEY, RASPBERRY ... SORRY, RAP–BERRY, SHOULDN'T YOU BE IN THE VEGETABLE SECTION? 'COS I HEARD YOU'RE *DOWN WITH THE BEETS!*

WHAT'S RED AND GREEN AND HOPS AROUND AUSTRALIA? *A KANGA-RHUBARB.*

HEY, STRAWBERRY, YOU SUCK! GET IT? BECAUSE YOU'RE A *STRAW-BERRY?* NYAH NYAH NYAH!

HA HA HA HA HA!

HEY! HEY, CORN! I HEARD YOU WERE ONCE IN THE ARMY – WEREN'T YOU *A KERNEL?*
WHAT'S YOUR FAVOURITE MUSIC, CORN – *IS IT POP?*
HEY, WHADDYA CALL CORN WHEN HE'S ON HIS OWN? *A UNICORN!*
A unicorn joke? I LOVE unicorns!
Oh, man ...
HEY, CUCUMBER! WHY *THE LONG FACE?*
CUCUMBER ALWAYS WEARS THE MOST AWESOME CLOTHES. HE'S SO COOL!

VEG OUT ONCE MORE!

POTATO'S ALWAYS GOT HIS EYES GLUED TO THE TV — HE'S A REAL *COUCH POTATO!*

HEY, POTATO! IF YOU WERE A DJ WOULD YOU PLAY *MASH-UPS?*

HEY! WHAT VEGETABLES GO BEST WITH JACKET POTATOES? *BUTTON MUSHROOMS!*

WHAT DO YOU CALL SOMETHING THAT'S SMALL, RED AND WHISPERS? A *HOARSE RADISH!* GET IT? HAHAHAHAHA!

SWEET POTATO WAS GOING TO START UP HIS OWN BUSINESS BUT UNFORTUNATELY ALL HIS IDEAS WERE *HALF-BAKED* ... HA HA HA!

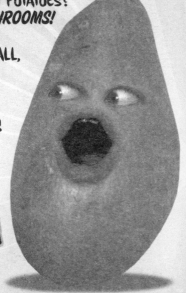

WAZZUUUP!

SWEDE'S ALWAYS RUNNING LATE.
YOU NEVER KNOW WHEN HE'S GOING TO *TURNIP*.

TOMATO! HEY, TOMATO, GOOD TO SEE YA! I WAS HOPING WE COULD *KETCHUP!* GET IT? KETCHUP? HAHAHA!
WHY AREN'T YOU LAUGHING?

Dude, how many more times? I don't belong on the vegetable pages. I'm a fruit! Tomatoes are fruits!

HEY TOMATO!

Wow, you're a puree of sunshine! Hahahaha!

HEY, TOMATO, IF YOU'RE REALLY A *FRUIT*, WHAT KIND OF FRUIT ARE YOU? ARE YOU A *CHERRY* TOMATO*?* OR A *PLUM* TOMATO*?*

I RECKON TOMATO GOT PUT IN THE BLENDER, AND NOW HE'S A LITTLE M/X_ED UP.

ANNOYING ORANGE'S FAVOURITE FILMS

Luckily these films are all really good, otherwise someone might have thrown me at the screen!

FINDING NACHO

BACK TO THE FRUITURE

ICE SAGE

TEENAGE MUTANT NINJA TURNIPS

NANNY MCPEA

JURASSIC PORK

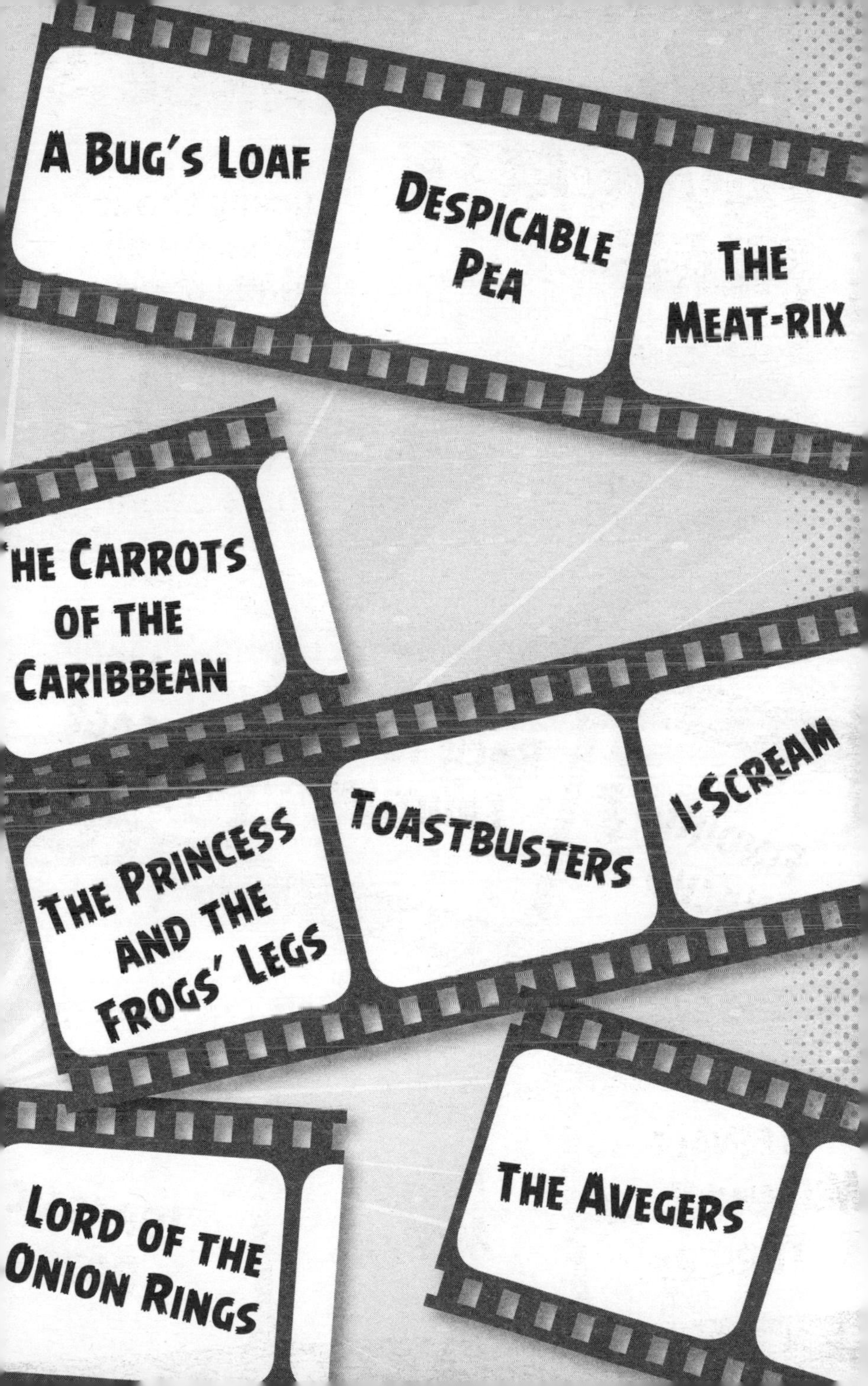

A Bug's Loaf

Despicable Pea

The Meat-rix

'he Carrots of the Caribbean

The Princess and the Frogs' Legs

Toastbusters

I-Scream

Lord of the Onion Rings

The Avegers

CHILL OUT!

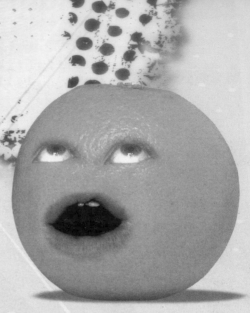

HEY! DID YOU HEAR THE GOSSIP ABOUT BUTTER? I BETTER NOT TELL YOU, YOU'LL JUST *SPREAD IT*. NO! I MEAN IT! DON'T TRY *BUTTERING ME UP!*

HEY, BUTTER! YOU LOOK EXHAUSTED. HAVE YOU BEEN *SPREADING YOURSELF TOO THIN?* HAHAHA!

HEY! WHAT'S A PIRATE'S FAVOURITE CHEESE? IT'S CHEDD-*AAAAAAARGH!*

Oh, dairy me!

HEY YOU!

HEY, HEY CHEESE! YOU'RE LOOKING GRATE! HAVE YOU *CHEDDAR* FEW POUNDS? HAHAHAHA!

HEY, CHEESE, DO YOU LIKE CHEESY MUSIC, OR ARE YOU MORE INTO *R'N'BRIE*?

WHAT DO YOU CALL CHEESE THAT IS SAD?
BLUE CHEESE!

AND WHAT DO YOU CALL CHEESE THAT DOESN'T BELONG TO YOU?
NACHO CHEESE! HAHAHAHA!

HEY!

Oh, VERY mature.

WHO CUT THE CHEESE?

KEEP COOL!

These egg jokes will really CRACK you up! Or should I say, these egg YOLKS? HA!

HEY, EGG, DON'T BE BASHFUL — COME OUT OF YOUR *SHELL!*

EGG'S A GOOD LOSER — HE ALWAYS KNOWS WHEN HE'S BEEN *BEATEN.*

HEY, HEY, EGG! IF YOU WORE A KILT YOU'D BE A *SCOTCH EGG!*

EGG TRIED TO SET UP A TV IN THE FRIDGE, BUT THE SIGNAL GOT *SCRAMBLED!* GET IT? HAHAHAHA!

HEY! HEY! HEY!

HOW DO YOU MAKE A CREAM PUFF? *CHASE IT ROUND THE KITCHEN!*

HEY, HEY MILK! WHAT DO YOU GET FROM NERVOUS COWS? *MILK SHAKE!*

SALAD CREAM JUST TOLD ME TO CLOSE THE FRIDGE DOOR ... *SHE'S DRESSING!* HAHAHA!

MILK

OMG

MEAT AND GREET!

Fowl Play

HEY! HEY, YOU! WHEN IS A CHICKEN LIKE A GUITAR?
WHEN IT'S BEEN *PLUCKED!*

WHAT'S THE NOISIEST PART OF A CHICKEN?
THE DRUMSTICK!

MAN, THAT CHICKEN'S A REALLY TOUGH AUDIENCE. GUESS SHE MUST
HAVE COME FROM A *HARD-BOILED EGG!*

HEY, WHAT DO YOU CALL THE GHOST OF A CHICKEN?
A POULTRY-GEIST!

HEY! HEY, TURKEY, AREN'T YOU HUNGRY? NO?
OH. YOU'RE *ALREADY STUFFED.*

HEY, TURKEY! I HOPE YOU DIDN'T *GOBBLE YOUR FOOD!*

MEAT AND GREET!

The Steaks are High

HEY, WHAT DO YOU CALL MEAT THAT LIKES TO MAKE CAKES? *BACON!*

HEY, BACON! YOU DON'T STILL HAVE THAT NASTY *RASH*, DO YOU? I REALLY HOPE *YOU'RE CURED!*

NYAH, NYAH, NYAH

WHAT'S THE DIFFERENCE BETWEEN ROAST BEEF AND PEA SOUP? ANYONE CAN *ROAST BEEF* ... HAHAHA!

HEY! HOW DO YOU STOP MEATBALL FROM DROWNING? PUT HIM IN A *GRAVY BOAT!*

HEY, WHAT DO YOU CALL LOTS OF MEATBALLS
FALLING FROM THE SKY?
A MEAT-EOR SHOWER!

HAHA HA HA HA!

HEY, PORK, I'M GLAD YOU DON'T DO KARATE. I WOULDN'T WANT
TO FEEL YOUR *PORK CHOP* ...

HEY! HEY, HEY! HOW DO YOU MAKE A SAUSAGE ROLL?
PUSH HIM OFF THE TABLE!

HEY, SAUSAGE! WHAT'S THE *WURST* SAUSAGE
JOKE YOU KNOW? *HAHA!*
SEE WHAT I DID THERE?

HEY, WHY IS SAUSAGE RUDE?
BECAUSE HE *SPITS* AT PEOPLE
WHEN HE'S COOKING!

NYAH, NYAH, NYAH

GONE FISHING

Hey! What happened to the shark who swallowed a bunch of keys? He got lockjaw! **Hahahaha!**

WHY DON'T FISH GO ON COMPUTERS? THEY'RE FRIGHTENED OF *THE NET!*

I've haddock up to here with your jokes and my patience is wearing fin!

HAHAHAHAHA
HAHAHAHAHAHA
HAHAHAHAHAHA

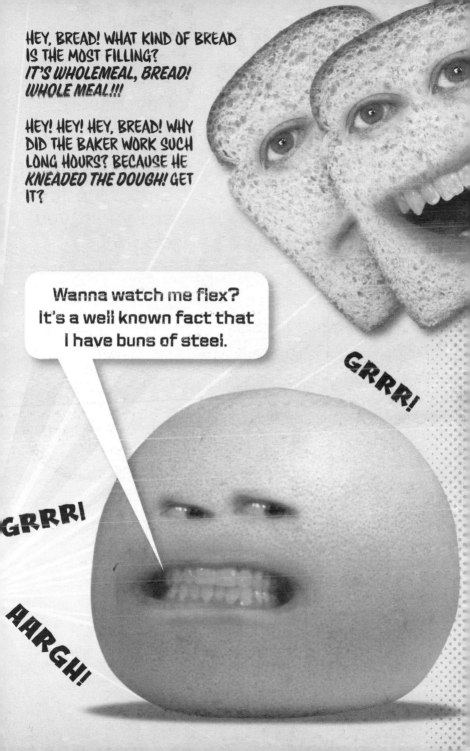

FLAKY PASTRIES

HEY! DID YOU HEAR ABOUT THE MAN WHO ATE FIFTEEN PANCAKES FOR BREAKFAST? OH, *HOW WAFFLE!*

HEY, CURRANT BUN, *YOU'RE ELECTRIC!*

HEY! WHICH TREE CAN YOU EAT? *PASTRY!* HAHAHA!

HEY, DONUT! IF YOU NEED A FILLING, YOU SHOULD *GO TO THE DENTIST!* HAHAHA!

GOIN' NUTS

HEY, GUESS WHAT KIND OF NUT MAKES A CHOCOLATE BAR? *A COCOA-NUT!* GET IT?

WHAT DO YOU CALL A NUT IN A SPACESHIP? *AN ASTRO-NUT!* HAHAHA!

What kind of nut always has a cold?

Sigh A cashew.

Bless you!

GRR!!

SHELF-CENTRED

You'll want to devour these books!

THE INVISIBLE FLAN

ANNE OF GREEN BAGELS

BLACKBERRY BEAUTY

WATERCRESS DOWN

GREAT EGGSPECTATIONS

HIS DARK CHOCOLATE MATERIALS

FOODIE AND THE FEAST

GOODNIGHT MISTER TOMATO

THE LUNCHBOX OF NOTRE DAME

THE JUNGLE COOK

LORD OF THE FRIES

THE FAMOUS CHIVE

HARRY POTPIE AND THE DEATHLY MARROWS

PETER PANCAKES

GREEN EGGS AND YAM

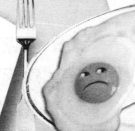

THE SPICE OF LIFE

HEY TOMATO!

You should take these with a grain of salt ...

HEY, WHICH HERB IS THE CLEVEREST? IT'S *SAGE!* HAHA!

HEY, HEY, SALT! *WHAT'S SHAKIN'?*

NYAH, NYAH, NYAH, NYAH

HEY, PEPPER! YOU'RE GETTING *RIGHT UP MY NOSE!*

HEY, BASIL, I WISH YOU'D STOP HANGING OUT WITH PARMESAN. YOU'RE *MAKING A REAL PESTO YOURSELF!*

PARSLEY JUST GOT A PAIR OF GLASSES –
HE WENT TO THE OPTICIAN AND FOUND OUT
HE WAS *PARSLEY-SIGHTED.*

MMM

WHAT'S GREEN AND SINGS ROCK 'N' ROLL?
ELVIS PARSLEY! GET IT? HAHAHA!

HEY, HEY THYME! IF YOU SPILLED ALL OVER ME, PEOPLE
WOULD SAY I HAD TOO MUCH THYME ON MY HANDS!
OH, EXCEPT I DON'T ACTUALLY HAVE HANDS...

GRRR!

GRRR!

Don't ask me to tell any more herbs and spices jokes. I'm done! No, I'm sorry, that's my fennel word.

AARGH!

HOW REFRESHING!

Hey! Let's wash those spicy jokes down with some refreshing drink jokes!

HEY, DID YOU HEAR THAT APPLE GOT HIT IN THE HEAD WITH A FIZZY DRINKS CAN? HE'S FINE – IT WAS ONLY A *SOFT DRINK!*

HEY, ORANGE JUICE! DID YOU HEAR ABOUT THE GUY WHO GOT CANNED FROM HIS JOB AT THE ORANGE JUICE FACTORY? *HE COULDN'T CONCENTRATE!*

WHY DID APPLE CRY?
SOMEONE HURT HIS
PEELINGS! HAHAHA!

HEY, GRANDPA LEMON!
IF YOU FALL OFF YOUR
MOTORCYCLE, WE'LL GIVE YOU
SOME *LEMON-AID!* HAHAHAHA!

Eh! What?

HEY, I JUST SAW LOADS
OF FIZZY DRINKS CANS
BEING SQUASHED FOR
RECYCLING. IT WAS
SODA-PRESSING!

HEY, COLA! CAN I GIVE
YOU A *POP QUIZ?*

HEY, WHERE DID
LEMONADE TAKE COLA?
TO A *POP CONCERT!*
POP! HAHA!

FAST FOOD FUNNIES

I'm going to knock these out of the park on the first fry!

HEY! IS IT CALLED FAST FOOD 'COZ YOU HAVE TO EAT IT *FAST* SO YOU *DON'T TASTE IT! IS IT? IS IT? IS IT?*

HOW DO YOU MAKE A HAMBURGER LAUGH? *GIVE IT A LITTLE PICKLE!*

WHAT DID THE HAMBURGER SAY TO THE PICKLE? YOU'RE *DILL-ICIOUS!*

HEY, ONION RINGS! WHICH ONE OF YOU IS THE RINGLEADER? ¡HAHAHA!

HEY! HOW DO YOU MEND A BROKEN PIZZA? *WITH TOMATO PASTE!* HAHA!

HEY, PIZZA! EVERYONE ALWAYS LAUGHS AT YOUR JOKES. IT MUST BE BECAUSE YOU HAVE SUCH GOOD *DELIVERY!*

HEY, DID YOU HEAR ABOUT THE SHEEP WHO WORKED IN THE FISH AND CHIP SHOP? YEAH, THEY WERE *BATTERING RAMS!* HAHAHA!

HEY, YOU! DO YOU KNOW WHERE FRENCH FRIES ARE MADE? *IN GREECE!* GET IT? HAHA!

JUST DESSERTS

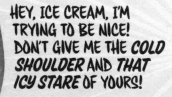

I love desserts! I love ice cream, and sprinkles, and custard, and crumble, and pudding!

HEY! HEY, ICE CREAM! *WHAT'S THE SCOOP?* HAHAHAHAHA!

THAT'S A NICE HAT, ICE CREAM – *IS THAT AN ICE CAP?*

HEY, ICE CREAM! DO YOU LIKE YOUR HOT DOGS WITH *CHILLY SAUCE?*

HEY, ICE CREAM, I'M TRYING TO BE NICE! DON'T GIVE ME THE *COLD SHOULDER* AND *THAT ICY STARE* OF YOURS!

OH NO! MARSHMALLOW FELL INTO THE FREEZER! MARSHMALLOW'S *OUT COLD!*

HEY! WHAT DO YOU CALL SOMEONE WITH CUSTARD IN ONE EAR AND JELLY IN THE OTHER? *A TRIFLE DEAF!* HAHAHA!

Hmm, I wonder what other dessert puns I can **cobble** together...

Sheesh, these jokes are getting difficult to **digest!**

SWEET NOTHIN'S

Oh no! I've eaten too many sweets! I've DESSERT-ED my diet! They've made me THICK to my stomach!

HEY, CHOCOLATE! THERE'S A ROCKY ROAD AHEAD, BUT THAT'S NO REASON TO HAVE A *MELTDOWN! HARDEN UP!*

HEY, ROCKY ROAD! ARE YOU BEST SERVED *STONE* COLD? HAHAHA!

HEY, CHOCOLATE BAR! IF I EAT HALF DARK CHOCOLATE AND HALF WHITE CHOCOLATE, DOES THAT COUNT AS A *BALANCED DIET?*

HEY, GUMMY WORM, ARE YOU CALLED GUMMY BECAUSE YOU HAVE *NO TEETH?* HAVE YOU *GROUND* THEM ALL DOWN? HAHAHAHA! GET IT? BECAUSE WORMS LIVE *IN THE GROUND?*

THAT MARSHMALLOW'S OUT OF THIS WORLD — A *MARTIAN-MALLOW,* SOME MIGHT SAY!

HEY, IF YOU SELL LOADS OF SWEETS, DO YOU MAKE *A MINT?*

HEY, MINT! IF YOU ROLLED OFF THE COUNTER YOU'D BE IN A REAL *PREDICA-MINT!* BUT THEN AGAIN, MAYBE YOU'D BE OK, YOU'VE ALWAYS BEEN VERY *DETER-MINT* ...

THAT TAKES THE BISCUIT!

HEY, COOKIE! KNOW ANY GOOD BISCUIT JOKES? I KNOW A FEW *CRACKERS!* HAHA!

HEY, COOKIE, WHY ARE YOU UPSET? DID YOU JUST BREAK UP WITH YOUR GIRLFRIEND? HAS SHE BEEN *A WAFER* TOO LONG? HAHAHAHAHA!

HEY, HEY COOKIE! WHAT'S THE MATTER? *CRUMBS,* YOU LOOK LIKE YOU'RE ABOUT TO *GO TO PIECES!*

HEY, COOKIE, YOU LOOK LIKE YOU'VE GOT A *CHIP* ON YOUR SHOULDER! YEAH, A *CHOCOLATE CHIP!* HAHA!

HEY, BISCUIT! YOU SHOULD PLAY BASKETBALL, 'COZ YOU'RE REALLY GOOD AT *DUNKING!*

HEY, WHAT KIND OF KEYS DO KIDS LIKE TO CARRY AROUND? *COOKIES!* HAHAHA!

I'VE EATEN SO MANY BISCUITS THAT I CAN'T *MACAROON* FOR ANY MORE! AND NOW I'M HAVING *DIGESTIVE* ISSUES!

HMM. I WOULD TELL YOU MY OTHER BISCUIT JOKE, BUT I THINK IT'S A BIT *CRUMBY* ... HAHAHA!

CUTTING REMARKS

These cutlery jokes are really **cutting edge!**

WHAT DID FORK SAY TO KNIFE? *LOOK SHARP!*

WHAT DID KNIFE SAY TO FORK? DO YOU WANT TO TAKE ANOTHER *STAB* AT DINNER?

WHAT ELSE DID KNIFE SAY TO FORK? WHAT'S *PRONG* WITH YOU? HAHAHA!

GRUESOME GIGGLES

As you know, everyone I talk to just gets chopped up, which has given me lots of ideas for gruesome giggles!

HEY! WHAT DID THE CHEESE GRATER SAY TO THE CHEESE? HE SAID, *"I'M GRATE!"*

WHEN ANOTHER ORANGE JUMPED IN THE BLENDER, I COULD SEE IT TOOK *LOTS OF GUTS.* HAHAHA!

WHEN POTATO MET PEELER, IT WAS A *FACE-OFF!* I DIDN'T KNOW WHO TO *ROOT* FOR! GET IT?

HEY, HEY KIWIS! I HEAR YOU'RE GOING TO BE IN A SMOOTHIE! I HOPE YOU'LL *BLEND* IN...

KNIFE

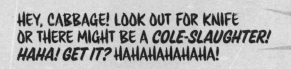
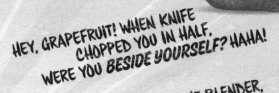

OMG! IT'S A MEDIA FRENZY!

JUICY GOSSIP

CELEBS!

APPLE'S PUBLIC OUTBURST — WE GET TO THE *CORE* OF THE STORY

JAM UNABLE TO *PRESERVE* DIGNITY AFTER LEAKED PHOTOS

OMG

COOKIE *CRUMBLES* UNDER PRESSURE

KNOCK KNOCK!
WHO'S THERE?
ICE CREAM!
ICE CREAM WHO?
ICE CREAM IF YOU DON'T LET ME IN!

KNOCK KNOCK!
WHO'S THERE?
BUTTER!
BUTTER WHO?
BUTTER WEAR YOUR COAT, IT'S COLD OUT HERE!

KNOCK KNOCK!
WHO'S THERE?
WAFER!
WAFER WHO?
WAFER A WHILE, BUT NOW I'M BACK!

KNOCK KNOCK!
WHO'S THERE?
JUSTIN!
JUSTIN WHO?
JUSTIN TIME FOR DINNER!

KNOCK KNOCK!
WHO'S THERE?
PASTA!
PASTA WHO?
PASTA FOOD, I'M STARVING!

KNOCK KNOCK!
WHO'S THERE?
PEAS!
PEAS WHO?
PEAS OPEN THE DOOR, I'M FROZEN!

ANNOYING ORANGE'S TOP TEN MOST ANNOYING JOKES OF ALL TIME

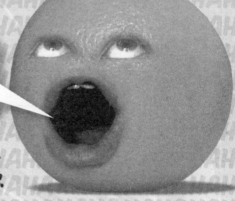

These jokes actually managed to annoy ME!

10 DOCTOR, YOUR JOKES ARE REALLY PAINFUL ... HMM, IT MUST BE THE *PUNCHLINES.*

9 TWO HATS WERE HANGING AROUND ON A SHELF. ONE SAID TO THE OTHER, "YOU STAY HERE, I'LL GO ON *AHEAD.*"

AARGH!

8 WHY CAN'T A BICYCLE STAND UP ON ITS OWN? BECAUSE IT'S *TWO-TYRED!*

OK, that one's quite good...

7 I WONDERED WHY THE FOOTBALL KEPT GETTING BIGGER. *THEN IT HIT ME.*

6 POLICE WERE CALLED TO A NURSERY THE OTHER DAY – APPARENTLY ONE OF THE THREE YEAR OLDS WAS *RESISTING A REST.*

5 I USED TO HAVE A FEAR OF HURDLES, BUT THEN I *GOT OVER IT.*

4 SEVEN DAYS WITHOUT FOOD MAKES *ONE WEAK.*

GRRR!

3 I'M GOOD FRIENDS WITH 25 LETTERS OF THE ALPHABET. I DON'T KNOW *y.*

2 I USED TO BE A TAP DANCER, UNTIL I FELL IN *THE SINK.*

And finally, the most annoying joke I've EVER heard...

1 THIS BOY I KNOW WAS TAKEN TO HOSPITAL BECAUSE HE SWALLOWED SOME COINS. WHEN HIS MUM CALLED TO ASK HOW HE WAS, THE DOCTOR SAID "NO *CHANGE* YET!"

MMM

Noooo! No more, I beg you!

GRRR!

OK, you have to stop now! This is ridiculous!

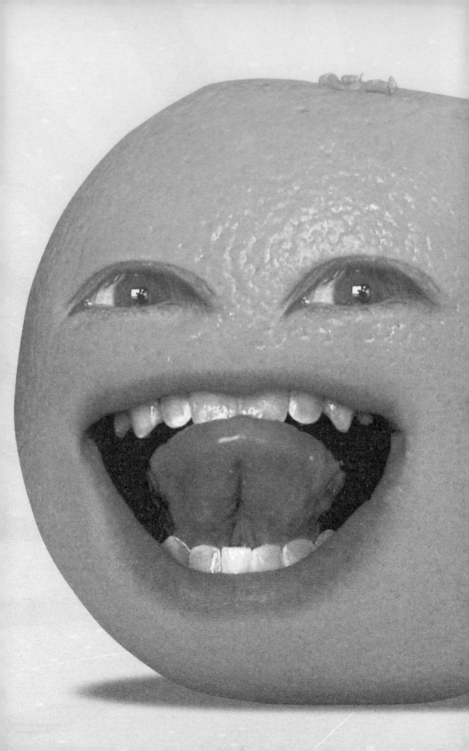